SPACE Audiation

Edwin E. Gordon

SPACE Audiation

Edwin E. Gordon
Research Professor
Thomas Cooper Library
University of South Carolina

G-8934

GIA Publications, Inc.
Chicago

About my sculpture and wall hangings—

I attempt to give an illusion of continuous free flowing movement in frozen captured space. This is accomplished by using textured vectors in silent harmonic interactions in the same way musicians use chords in space audiation improvisation.

Space Audiation
Edwin E. Gordon

G-8934
ISBN: 978-1-62277-140-0

7404 S. Mason Ave
Chicago IL 60638

www.giamusic.com

Printed in the United States of America

Contents

Preface

Concise concepts presented in this monograph are speculative though not spontaneous. They have been roaming my mind vaguely for many years, coherently only on rare occasions. The main problem was I could not always find appropriate words to explain my thinking in a simple and clear manner. At first the concepts seemed sensational. The further thought I devoted to them, however, the more ordinary they became. My mission, still searching for a few remaining relevant words, is to express my thoughts plainly to readers for serious consideration. Perhaps the quest for words is necessary because I am without objective research to support the concepts. Although I have made considerable progress in my pursuit, I still am somewhat constricted by use of the words space, distance, time, and silence. Nonetheless, I make distinctions between auditory space and physical space and between music time and natural time as each interacts with movement. I have deduced silence for listeners comprises anticipation and prediction whereas for performers, space audiation surrounding the moment is the predominant factor.

I do not embrace the belief the hypotheses will be accepted, if ever, totally by music educators and practicing and academic musicians. I write to alleviate boredom and because I believe the observations must be expressed. Perhaps I am writing for myself rather than others. Nonetheless, the views may encourage music professionals to think about music learning in novel ways. The concepts undoubtedly will not be used, if at all, in complete format as presented. When given sincere reflection, I envisage they will modify somewhat music teaching pedagogy. Any change from stifling and repressive tradition will be a compelling improvement.

Approaching my 88th birthday and my health not being the best, this will probably be my final work. It represents assimilation and culmination of selected material found in my books, research monographs, and test manuals. If I do a creditable job, it could be preeminent. It is purposely condensed so it quickly may be reviewed several times. Take time to read, reread, and think over a period of time about the concepts. They will tend to grow on you. It took me many years to comprehend the conceivable importance and compelling nature of the perspectives.

Introduction

The word audiation came into existence in 1975 as a footnote in an early book on music learning theory. Coining the word was necessary to conduct research and explain how music is given meaning by persons of all ages. Aural perception and imagery, for example, offer limited insight into how the mind processes music. Audiation, in comparison, is comprehensive. Use of audiation in various venues has become widespread. Additionally, its significance has been expanded into an entire chapter in *Music Learning Sequences: A Contemporary Music Learning Theory*.

In the initial conception of audiation, I was unaware of the integral importance of space audiation and, thus, I unfortunately gave it minimal consideration. My current purpose is to amend that omission. To be thorough, it is essential I briefly review a description of classical audiation without negating any part but expanding its totality.

Sound itself is not music. Sound becomes music through audiation when, as with language, sounds are translated in the mind and given meaning. Meaning given these sounds is different depending on the occasion as well as different from meaning given them by other persons. Audiation is the process of assimilating and comprehending (not simply rehearing) music heard in the immediate past or days, weeks, months, or years ago. Musicians audiate also when assimilating and comprehending in their minds music that may or may not have been heard but is read in notation, composed, or improvised.

Aural perception takes place when sound is reacted to without comprehension the moment it is produced. Sound is audiated only after it is aurally perceived. In aural perception, persons are dealing with immediate sound events. In audiation they are attending to delayed musical events. Moreover, compared to what is often called musical imagery, audiation is a more profound process. Musical imagery casually suggests a vivid or figurative picture of what music might represent. It does not require assimilation and comprehension of intrinsic elements of music as does audiation.

Audiation may occur when listening to, recalling, performing, interpreting, creating, improvising, reading, and writing music. Though it may seem contradictory, persons can listen to music while at the same audiating music. Most persons automatically think about what has been said and predict what will be said while at the same time listening to or participating in conversation. Listening to music with comprehension and listening to speech with comprehension involve similar operations. Further, in notational audiation, as you will begin to give meaning to words you are reading now only after you have read them, you give meaning to music notation not as but only after you have seen it.

Consider language, speech, and thought. Language is the result of need to communicate. Speech is how we communicate. Thought is what we communicate. Music, performance, and audiation have parallel meanings. Music is the subject of communication. Performance is the vehicle for communication. Audiation is what is communicated. Although music is not a language, the process is the same for audiating and giving meaning to music as for thinking and giving meaning to speech.

When listening to speech we give meaning to what was said by recalling and making connections with what was heard immediately before. At the same time we are anticipating or predicting what will be heard next based on experience and understanding. Similarly, when listening to music we give meaning to what was newly heard by recalling what was heard on earlier occasions. At the same time we are anticipating or predicting what we will be hearing next based on music achievement. In other words, when we are audiating as we are listening to music we are summarizing and generalizing content of music patterns in its confirmed context as a way to anticipate or predict what will follow. Every action becomes an interaction. What we are audiating depends on what we have audiated. As audiation develops, it becomes broader and deeper and, thus, reflects more on itself.

Some musicians are capable of audiating one piece of music while listening to or performing another. Others are capable of audiating inner and lower parts of music while they are audiating its melody. Musicians who are improvising a melody may comprehensively audiate chords underlying a melody or a melody that embellishes an established chord progression. Jazz instrumentalists, scat singers, rap, and blue grass performers may audiate a phrase from one piece of music and substitute it for the original phrase in music they are performing. They, like some, may not be able to explain in technical or theoretical terms what they are audiating. Whereas most musicians who perform jazz through imitation can perform in only one style, those who audiate can comfortably perform jazz in two or more styles; for example, both swing and bebop. Composers who audiate, those who are not steadfastly dependent on an instrument while composing, simultaneously audiate several components of music they are creating, such as melody, harmony, phrasing, and instrumentation.

Audiation, as opposed to imitation which is a preliminary step in developing audiation potential, are often confused. Imitation, sometimes called inner hearing, is a product whereas audiation is a process. It is possible and unfortunately too often the case music is performed by imitation without engaging in audiation. It is not possible to imitate and audiate at the same time. Learning by rote is not the same as learning with understanding, whether the subject be history, mathematics, or music.

Like imitation, memory (not memorization) and recognition are part of audiation processes. Alone, however, they are not audiation. Persons can recognize music even when it is performed with some incorrect pitches and durations and still not be able to audiate it. They might be aware of at most only its melodic contour and rhythm. Many persons who recognize "Jingle Bells" are unable to sing its resting tone, to identify and move to its fundamental beats, to hear its tonality and meter, or to specify chord progressions underlying its melody.

Most students and probably as many musicians memorize music without audiating contextually. Memorizing music on an instrument is primarily related to fingerings and other technical matters, not to audiation. Many persons who can play a melody on an instrument are unable to sing what they have played; to play a variation of the original melody; to play the melody in a different keyality, tonality, or meter; to play the melody with alternate fingerings; or to demonstrate with body movement phrases of the melody. If they cannot do these things they are not audiating what they have performed. It is as if they were reciting words they had memorized without ascribing meaning to them.

Rhythm Theory

A brief presentation of rhythm theory is necessary to understand the role of space in performing and reading rhythm notation. Feeling of space is crucial for listening to and performing music to conceive and appropriate macrobeats and microbeats as they support rhythm patterns in usual and unusual meters. They also provide foundation for space in tonal and expressive elements. Explanations of important elements of rhythm follow.

Usual Meter

Three components that define rhythm are macrobeats, microbeats, and rhythm patterns. They are audiated concurrently to establish rhythm context in usual and unusual meters. Measure signatures are arbitrary in all examples. For supplementary information, read *Learning Sequences in Music: A Contemporary Music Learning Theory*, *Rhythm: Contrasting the Implications of Audiation and Notation*, *The*

Aural/Visual Experience of Music Literacy, *Improvisation in the Music Classroom,* and *Harmonic Improvisation for Adult Musicians.* All are published by GIA.

Macrobeats

Although not all persons will identify the same beats as longest, whichever beats felt to be longest are called macrobeats. Macrobeats are fundamental to feeling microbeats and rhythm patterns, because microbeats and rhythm patterns are superimposed on macrobeats in audiation. Following are examples of macrobeats in usual meter,

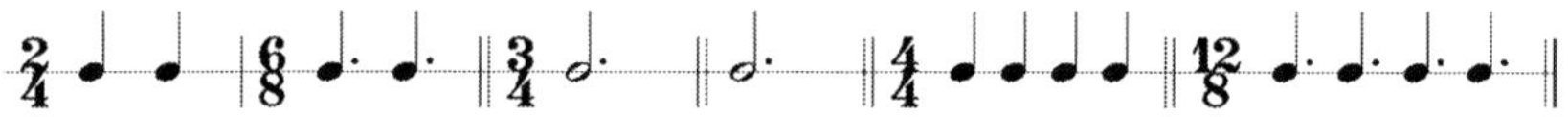

Microbeats

Microbeats are shorter than macrobeats and are derived from equal division of macrobeats. When macrobeats are divided into two microbeats of equal length, the first of two coinciding with a macrobeat, the result is usual duple meter. When macrobeats are divided into three microbeats of equal length, the first of three coinciding with a macrobeat, the result is usual triple meter. When some macrobeats are divided into two microbeats of equal length and other macrobeats are divided into three microbeats of equal length regardless of sequence of groupings, the result is usual combined meter. In usual combined meter, all macrobeats are of equal length but not all microbeats are of equal length.

Music is considered to be in usual meter only when macrobeats are audiated in pairs and are of equal length.

Following are examples of microbeats in usual duple meter, usual triple meter, and usual combined meter.

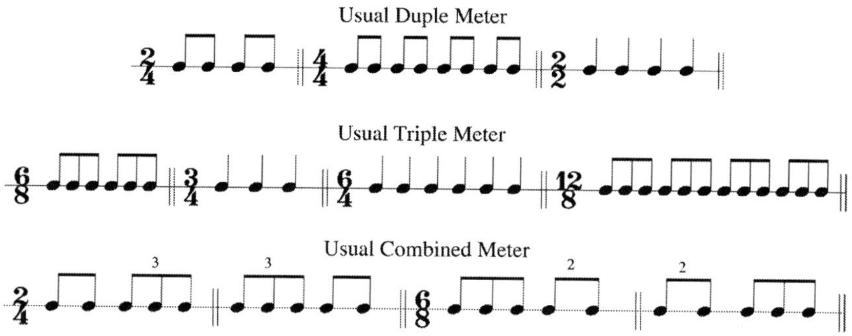

Rhythm Patterns

Text of melody incorporates one or a series of rhythm patterns. Typically, a rhythm pattern in usual meter is not shorter than one underlying macrobeat (which may include two or three underlying microbeats) and is no longer than two underlying macrobeats. Rhythm patterns, in addition to rests, ties, and upbeats, may include macrobeats, microbeats, divisions, and elongations of macrobeats and microbeats. Following are examples of rhythm patterns in usual duple meter, usual triple meter, and usual combined meter.

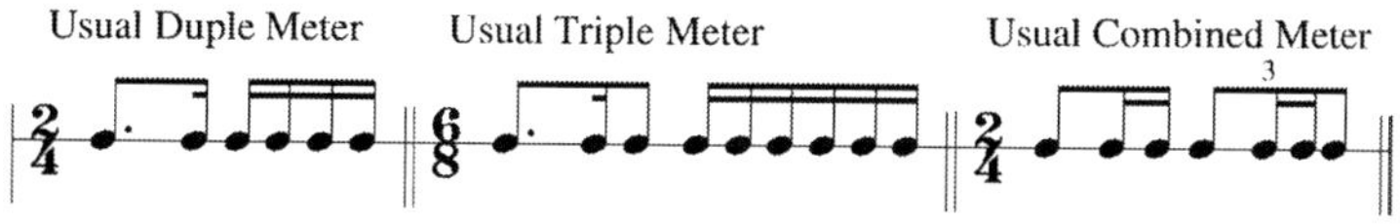

Following are examples in score form of macrobeats, microbeats, and rhythm patterns in the three usual meters: usual duple, usual triple, and usual combined.

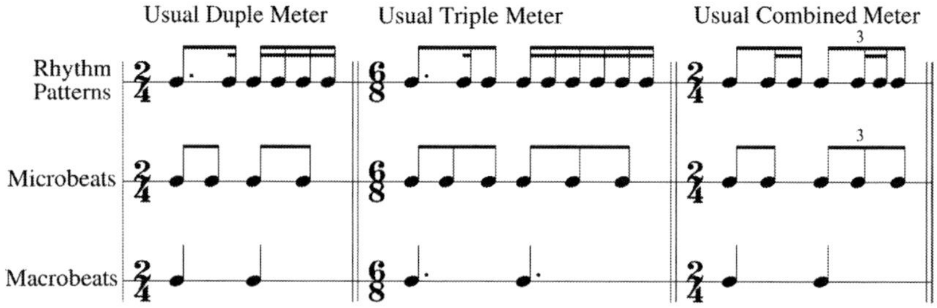

Unusual Meter

In usual duple and triple meters, all macrobeats and microbeats are of equal length. When macrobeats are not of equal length, music is in unusual meter. This is so whether one audiates macrobeats in pairs and regardless of their sequence. Because all macrobeats are not of equal length in unusual meter, some may be divided into two microbeats, others into three microbeats, and some may not be divided at all. That is, they may be intact. There are four types of unusual meter: unusual paired, unusual unpaired, unusual paired intact, and unusual unpaired intact.

Usual meter is determined by how macrobeats are divided in a rhythm pattern. Unusual meter is determined by how macrobeats are grouped in a rhythm pattern. It is number and relative lengths of macrobeats in a grouping that determine which type of unusual meter is being audiated.

When macrobeats are audiated in pairs in a rhythm pattern, meter is called unusual paired. It is paired because there are two macrobeats in a grouping. It is unusual because lengths of the two macrobeats are not equal. When macrobeats are not audiated in pairs, meter is called unusual unpaired, in this case because there are three macrobeats in a grouping and lengths of macrobeats are unequal. Although two of the three macrobeats form a pair in unusual unpaired meter, one macrobeat, the odd one, goes unpaired in the rhythm pattern. The listener, performer, or conductor subjectively decides through audiation which macrobeats, regardless of lengths, are paired and which are unpaired.

Macrobeats

Following are examples of macrobeats in unusual paired meter and unusual unpaired meter. Sequence of macrobeats of different lengths does not affect meter. It is uncommon for a sequence of macrobeats of different lengths to remain consistent from beginning to end in music in unusual meter.

Unusual Paired Meter

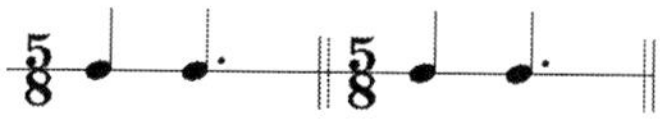

Unusual Unpaired Meter

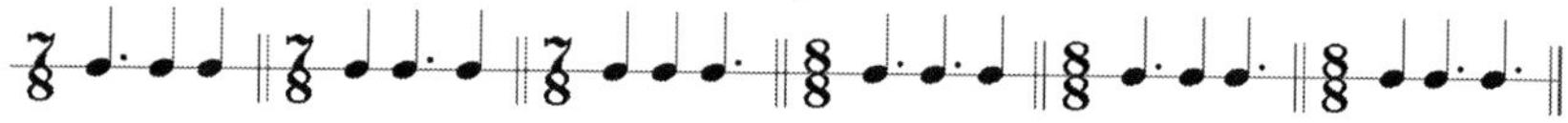

Microbeats

Following are examples of microbeats in unusual paired meter and unusual unpaired meter.

Unusual Paired Meter

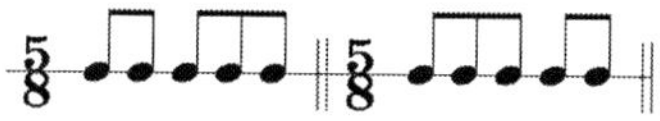

Unusual Unpaired Meter

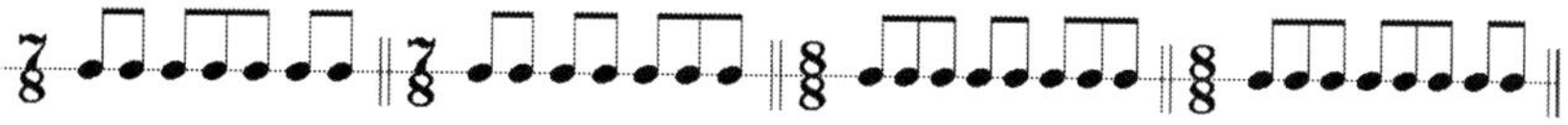

Rhythm Patterns

Following are examples of rhythm patterns in unusual paired meter and unusual unpaired meter.

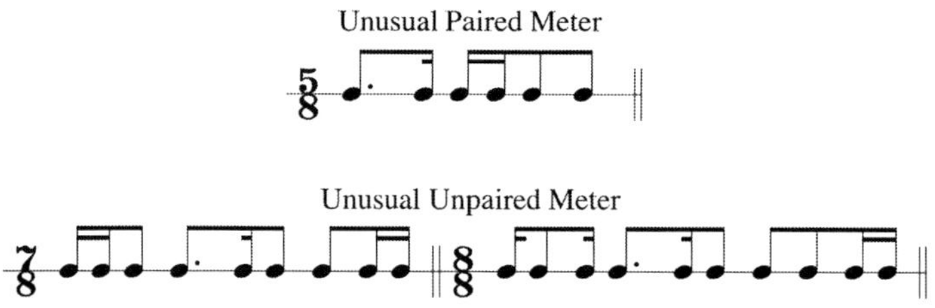

Following in score form are macrobeats, microbeats, and rhythm patterns in unusual paired meter and unusual unpaired meter.

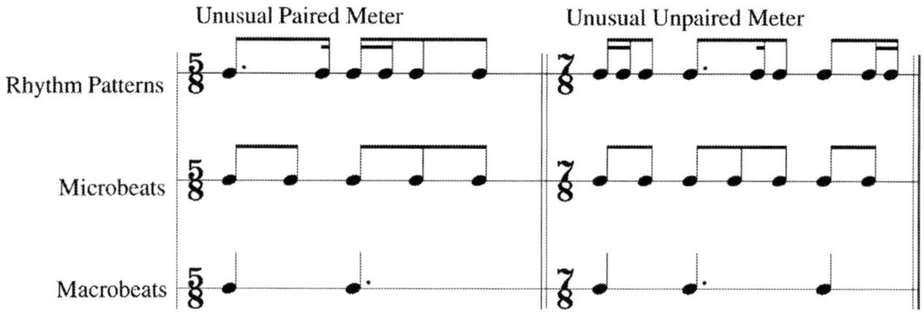

Unusual Intact Meter

Macrobeats

A macrobeat the length of only one microbeat is called an intact macrobeat. It is found in only unusual meter. Because an intact macrobeat is heard simultaneously with itself as its only microbeat, the two are concurrent in audiation and performance. Intact macrobeats may be divided into only divisions of microbeats.

When at least one intact macrobeat is in a rhythm pattern, the rhythm pattern is called intact. A rhythm pattern is in unusual paired intact meter when there are only two macrobeats in the pattern, one macrobeat being intact and the other not, and in unusual unpaired intact meter when there are three macrobeats in the pattern, either one or two but not all macrobeats being intact.

Intact macrobeats are found in combination with other longer macrobeats in a rhythm pattern divided into twos and threes or into only twos or only threes. A macrobeat may be paired with any other macrobeat, including another intact macrobeat, or it may not be paired. It is decided subjectively in audiation which macrobeats are paired and unpaired.

Following are examples of intact macrobeats in combination with macrobeats in unusual paired intact meter and unusual unpaired intact meter.

Unusual Paired Intact Meter

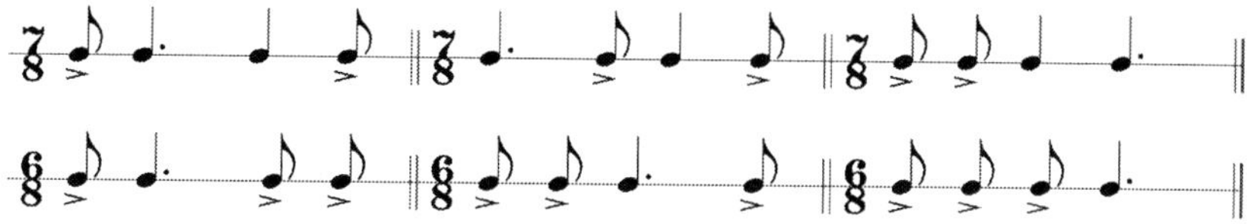

Unusual Unpaired Intact Meter

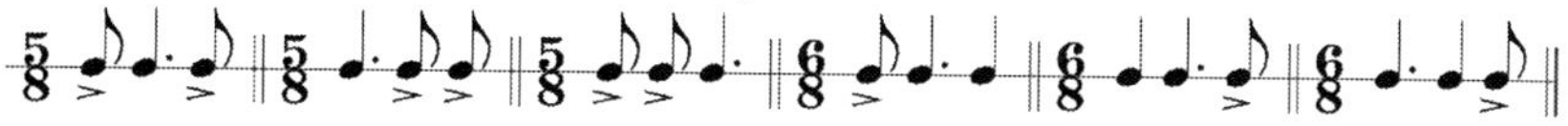

Microbeats

In the following examples of unusual paired and unpaired intact meters, intact macrobeats are flagged and microbeats are beamed. Macrobeats not intact are not included in the examples.

Unusual Paired Intact Meter

Unusual Unpaired Intact Meter

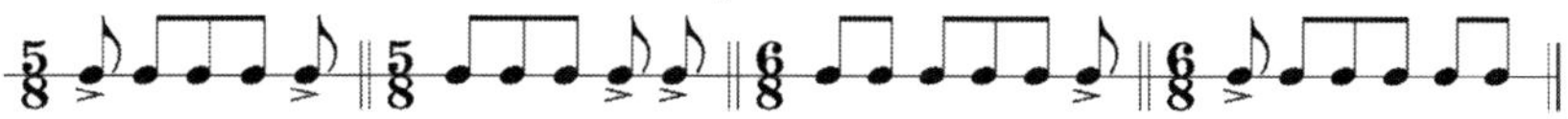

Rhythm Patterns

Following are examples of rhythm patterns in unusual paired and unusual unpaired intact meters. A rhythm pattern in unusual paired intact meter, which includes one intact macrobeat, is superimposed on two underlying macrobeats. A rhythm pattern in unusual unpaired intact meter, which includes one or two intact macrobeats, is superimposed on three underlying macrobeats. Type of unusual intact meter is determined by audiating underlying macrobeats and microbeats.

Unusual Paired Intact Meter

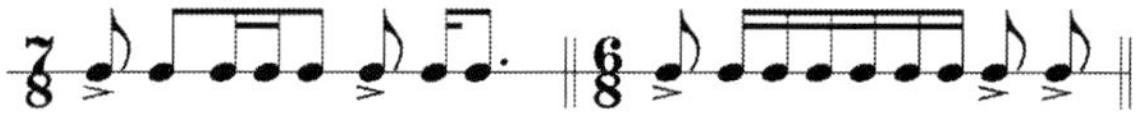

Unusual Unpaired Intact Meter

Following are examples in score form of intact macrobeats, macrobeats not intact, microbeats, and rhythm patterns notated in unusual paired intact meter and unusual unpaired intact meter.

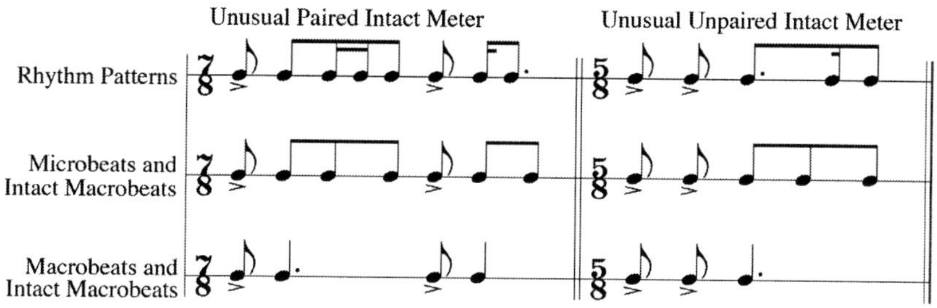
Unusual Paired Intact Meter
Unusual Unpaired Intact Meter
Rhythm Patterns
Microbeats and Intact Macrobeats
Macrobeats and Intact Macrobeats

Space Audiation in Rhythm

It has been a tradition to teach rhythm by presenting and defining what commonly are called time signatures and meter signatures (they are actually measure signatures) along with naming and counting note values. Such extraneous efforts and theoretical information alone have little if anything to do with music, particularly feeling of movement or spatial motion. Throughout history, individuals have attempted to moderate the effect of improper teaching of rhythm by describing various types of physical energy and recommending body movements be taught before theoretical information, if indeed theoretical information need be taught at all. No doubt innovations have made significant improvement in rhythm awareness of those who were fortunate to have been introduced to foundational rhythm physical activities before learning mentally to react to and count beats.

There is sufficient reason to believe, while not discounting importance of physical movement in developing a practical understanding of rhythm, audiation of heretofore unrecognized or unacknowledged motion in space is perhaps more advantageous. It is experienced as a silent auditory response rather than a physical response. The silent auditory response is efficaciously described as space audiation. It is interior motion in the mind as compared to exterior movement with the body. Whereas movement is ongoing predetermined and calculated action, motion and symbiotic (e)motion in conjunction with deep breaths are spontaneous and immediate. Space audiation is a template for accuracy and sensitivity in musical time.

To perform rhythm in an expressive musical manner, beats are not audiated linearly in natural or musical time. Macrobeats, microbeats, and rhythm patterns are audiated internally in the mind in circular motion without center or boundaries. The three essentials are superimposed simultaneously on one another. They momentarily are audiated expressively as a group of no specific phrase or section length and, thus, are not separately distinguishably. Meter, in terms of microbeats, however, is continually audiated and sustained unconsciously. In contrast, counting beat pulsations and reciting individual note names and values are nonfunctional. Imitating, memorizing, and rehearsing what will be performed, if attempted, defeats motion in space audiation.

Note values are best considered suggestions. For artistic performance, durations of notes are fluid, not frozen. When values are not taken literally or rendered precisely, resultant flexibility offers and creates exceptional opportunities for space audiation. It is detrimental for teachers and conductors to insist notes be given "full count."

Space audiation skills may be developed when performing with or without smusic notation but best when improvising. As a preliminary step, listening to and feeling what is intended to be performed is requisite. As a result, particulars of what will be performed occur unsurprisingly without forethought. The body usually moves in a free flowing, not absolute, manner without keeping time physically.

Use of a baton and metronome or tapping feet counteract development of space audiation. Dance as opposed to free flowing spatial movement is also a detriment to acquiring feeling for motion in space audiation. In routine music activities, conductors using regimented arm patterns and drummers who consistently perform loud microbeats are undesirable necessities for many persons. They keep physical time for listeners and performers who are incapable of doing it for themselves, never having given space audiation thought.

Consider language. Before speaking, you have a brief momentary synopsis of what you want to say. You do not think of sequence and order of every word or correct grammar. One word, nevertheless, follows another in constructive manner. In fact, most sentences are improvised. The same is true for audiating motion in space concurrently with music improvisation and reading performance.

Moreover, maintaining consistent tempo requires no special attention. One asset of space audiation is tempo remains stable while allowing for rubato in expressive interpretation. Rhythm elements, of course, interact with tonal elements in space audiation motion as explained in forthcoming chapters.

In conventional rhythm instruction, rests are taught as periods of silence. In space audiation, however, rests do not exist independently. When audiating space in performance, motion of rests is combined with macrobeats, microbeats, and rhythm patterns. They are integral extensions of beats and patterns that link and bind all three essentials together into a complete interconnected entity. Natural time separates beats whereas motion in space audiation connects and unifies them.

What are commonly thought of as rests are immersed in totality of rhythm and primarily are responsible for creating interpretation and phrasing of music. Meter and artistry in rhythm emerge not on distinct beats but in periods of continuous space that occur imperceptibly and unconsciously between macrobeats, microbeats, and rhythm patterns. That is manifest when performers are told to stop looking at notation. Instead, listen and feel. Then place notes in space where they offer sensitive artistic phrasing that results in series of subtle agogic accents. Though fashions in art are in constant change, style preserved in motion in space audiation remains constant.

Space audiation is most evident in improvisation. That is not to say, however, space audiation is not relevant when reading music notation or otherwise performing. The mind does not concentrate on only one rhythm pattern in natural time. The outmoded method of counting and thinking about individual beats and patterns one after the other undermines musicality. Patterns performed and those to be performed or omitted are audiated concurrently as they relate collectively in space to macrobeats and microbeats, all being linked in motion to one another. To strain to give musical meaning to a single rhythm patterns without reference to previous and forthcoming ones is strictly a mechanical process. Sensitive interpretation is cast aside.

Meter and tonality, whether sustained or modulatory, are ever present without effort in motion in auditory space as macrobeats, microbeats, rhythm patterns, and tonal patterns are combined by performers. Listeners respond attentively to resultant sounds of performers who are engaged in space audiation. The situation is clearly different for listening to contemporary music when misguided performers and composers have endeavored to reject tonality and meter. With regard to rhythm in so-called arrhythmic and atonal music, unfortunately counting and attending to separate beats and patterns is a necessity.

Space Audiation in Melody

To various degrees, everyone has five language vocabularies. In sequential order of development they are listening, speaking, thinking, reading, and writing. Historically, it is estimated there have been 30,000 languages spoken in the world. Presently, more or less than 6,000 remain. Why did so many language disappear? Linguists posit a language is no farther from extinction than only one skipped generation of adults not acculturating newborn and preschool children to that language.

There are five parallel sequential music vocabularies. Listening, singing/chanting, audiating/improvising, reading, and writing. As with a language listening vocabulary, extensive development of a music listening vocabulary is indispensible. It begins with newborns and continues throughout life. Without the fundamental music listening vocabulary established, at best skill in space audiation motion develops marginally.

With regard to music, the listening vocabulary instills the basis for feeling motion in space audiation as it combines tonal and rhythm elements. Nevertheless, space audiation in rhythm is the underpinning for overall motion in space audiation, and it provides a framework for phrasing.

Tonal patterns play a central role in melody space audiation. They are not audiated in linear fashion, one after the other. Tonal patterns in a section are audiated circularly and synchronously. When performed, space within tonal patterns is not uniform. Parallel tonal patterns and rhythm patterns in the same piece of music usually are not of similar length. Most tonal patterns are shorter or longer than associated rhythm patterns.

Just as meter is constantly audiated as background information, so is tonality. A specific objective tonality – such as major, minor, Dorian, Phrygian, Lydian, Mixolydian, and Aeolian – permeates and informs appropriate intonation with tonality modulations taken into consideration. In subjective tonality, a performer makes personal motion decisions in space audiation pertaining to if, how, and when tonality changes.

It is common belief poor intonation is a result of improper action of vocal folds in the throat. That is a misguided assumption. Accurate intonation ultimately is established in space audiation. Singing, however, is necessary preparation for acquiring decisive intonation in space audiation. When acceptable intonation is developed in terms of motion in space audiation, it naturally is transmitted to vocal folds. Without ability to sing in tune, instrumental as well as vocal intonation is uncertain and generally ambiguous.

There is, of course, no atonal music. All music must embrace one or more tonalities or it simply would constitute noise, not audiation. Multitonal and multikeyal music, erroneously referred to as atonal music, has rapidly changing tonalities and keyalities. In that a tonality gives rise to an objective syllabic resting tone (a note-name tonic), it, too, is sustained in background audiation as it complements tonality.

Common practice music theory emphasizes scales, intervals, and whole and half steps. That knowledge actually undermines development of motion in tonal space audiation because it emphasizes up and down direction. Specific attention to one dimensionality reduces possibility of acquiring multidimensional motion in spatial audiation.

With regard to naming notes and so-called key signatures, music theory errs in a unique manner. It accentuates linear organization to exclusion of comprehensive directional audiation. Names of individual notes offer as little meaning in audiating tonal patterns as memorizing the alphabet gives slight meaning to words. If key signatures were rightfully referred to as "do" signatures by music theorists (in practice, tonality determines the name of keyality), music theory would not be so troublesome.

Space Audiation in Harmony

It is customary when teaching common practice music theory to explain individual chord construction. For example, discussion of which pitches are in soprano and bass voices. Also, chord inversions take on prime importance. Emphasis is not on only individual chords but there is also concern for which pitches in a chord may or not be doubled. Avoidance of parallel motion is a routine obsession. Building chords vertically and separating individual parts defeats the concepts of motion in space audiation. A more sensible approach would be to study how chords interact with one another when moving horizontally. That would reinforce assimilating motion of chords in spatial audiation.

There are chords patterns and chord progressions. Patterns are integral in harmony whereas progressions are fundamental in advanced improvisation. Patterns typically include three chords (or triads) that are seen individually in notation but are audiated collectively. In space audiation there are no divisions between and among chords within a pattern. Thus, there is no sensing of linear movement in space audiation.

How chords are built vertically is of no relevance in space audiation. Ongoing chord patterns are heard as clusters, each representing various functions – such as tonic, dominant, and subdominant – that together enrich overall sonority. Although each chord in a pattern contributes to comprehensive sonority, none is audiated independently. All chords in a pattern are superimposed on one another and audiated circularly and synchronically in space audiation. Sonority of chord patterns contributes to sustaining a sense of tonality. It serves as preparation for audiating subsequent chord patterns and progressions.

What is called harmonic rhythm by music theorists is a vestige of historical music education. Space audiation of placement of chord patterns in music is guided by motion of tonal and rhythm patterns, not by ongoing macrobeats and microbeats audiated in strict musical time.

Space Audiation in Improvisation

There are various ways to improvise in traditional singing and instrumental performance. Three most popular approaches are 1) performing variations of a melody in the same or different styles, 2) performing scale patterns while reading chord symbols, and 3) performing original melodies superimposed on a progression of harmonic patterns or performing a progression of unique harmonic patterns that support a melody. In the first approach, musicians perform variations of a melody without necessarily being conscious of the progression of harmonic patterns that forms foundation of the melody. In the second, musicians perform melodic fragments based on scales associated with fixed single chords.

In the third approach, melody is improvised over a progression of harmonic patterns in much the same way it was done using figured bass during the Baroque, so progressions of harmonic patterns direct performers in improvising melody. Also, melody directs performers in improvising harmonic progressions. The harmonic progression approach requires motion in space audiation whereas the other two for the most part require imitation or memorization.

Furthermore, it has been discovered readiness for conventional improvisation has progressive characteristics. From least to most readiness is 1) not knowing chord changes have occurred, 2) knowing chord changes have occurred but not knowing the nature of the changes, 3) knowing chord changes have occurred and also knowing the nature of the changes, and 4) knowing chord pattern and progression changes have occurred, knowing the nature of the changes, and also predicting chord patterns and progressions that might collectively and logically follow. Motion in space audiation is integral to the fourth type.

In common practice harmony, harmonic patterns are fundamental. In space audiation improvisation, motion of harmonic progressions, which includes series of harmonic patterns, is basic. Rhythm patterns, tonal patterns, and harmonic patterns fused with harmonic progressions are audiated and move circularly and synchronically as a totality, not in linear fashion nor is one dominant over the other.

Consider how I was thinking when I wrote the previous sentence. The thought came all at once. As with speaking, I am not aware of individual words nor parts of a sentence. Harmonic progressions enter audiation in the same spatial way. Identification of individual chords and patterns contradicts, if not prevents, motion in space audiation.

Ability to audiate harmonic progressions cannot be taught directly in formal music instruction. Success in learning to audiate motion of harmonic progressions spatially requires significant informal preparation. Listening to many harmonic progressions and allowing sufficient time to comprehend relationships and differences among segments, without theorizing, may seem to take an inordinate amount of time. But that, as with language acquisition, is the reality. Books and teachers rarely help. What is particularly beneficial is attending to harmonic progressions in more than one style of music.

Awareness of sequence of macrobeats and microbeats audiated as background fabrics are without influence in determining motion of harmonic progressions in space audiation. They do, of course, assist in placement of complete harmonic progressions but not in consigning disconnected chords or harmonic patterns in rhythmic flow.

Space Audiation in Creativity

Creativity and improvisation share a few characteristics. Thus, creativity includes some improvisation and improvisation involves some creativity. A primary difference is whereas a composer reviews and makes changes and additions to a piece of music, improvisation is impromptu bereft of modification. There is, however, a more profound difference. Unlike in improvisation where chord progressions are joined, motifs in creativity are detached while being developed in circular motion in space audiation. Space between motifs is not uniform and does not move in ordinary musical time. Motifs are sustained in memory and later connected to create a unified whole. Rhythm, melody, harmony, interpretation, and instrumentation may be audiated simultaneously, in combinations, or separately regardless of musical style.

The compelling attribute creativity and improvisation have in common is neither is notated. What is finally created, nonetheless, may be notated but it may be assured two persons would not produce the same precise representations.

Subjectivity of scribes is to be expected. It is a result of unique templates in motion in space audiation. Creativity undertaken in space audiation provides most sensitive and artistic results when instruments are not used in the inventive process.

Space Audiation in Music Expression and Interpretation

There is a difference between space and silence in expression and interpretation of music. A performer audiates space whereas a listener construes it as silence. Space and silence occur between, around, and coincidental with macrobeats, microbeats, and rhythm patterns. It is the effect primarily of motion in space and silence between macrobeats and microbeats that produces musical sensitivity, particularly phrasing. In counterpoise and to a lesser extent, it is sustained phrasing across macrobeats and microbeats, essentially lack of space and silence, that also contributes to artistic and stylistic expression and interpretation in music. Significance of motion in space audiation is best manifested and most evident in tone quality, expression, and interpretation of music. It rarely becomes a reality without attention to rhythm, melody, harmony, and improvisation.

Music Notation

Music notation by itself is incomplete. It indicates lesser important elements of music. Dynamic markings and tempo markings only suggest how a composition is to be interpreted. Moreover, space audiation motion, which makes expression and interpretation in music possible as a result of not always giving some notes their precise value, cannot be indicated with accuracy or objectivity using music notation. That is why composers often need to explain to conductors during rehearsals of premier performances how their music is to be expressed. No one knows for sure how J. S. Bach actually intended his music to sound. Consider notational and spatial differences in interpretation of J. S. Bach's' *Goldberg Variations* by Glenn Gould and Andreas Schiff. What is seen in notation is incidental. Music is audiated. Music notation is read and written.

Musicians are expected to audiate everything they see in notation but because of imprecision of notation, they cannot be expected to put into notation everything they audiate.

Attempts to notate jazz are exemplary. Unless audiated, it cannot be expected music notation alone will ultimately impart musical meaning. Without audiation, musicians are destined to conjecture when reading music notation.

For example, many young pianists who cannot audiate use piano keys the way they do pitch letter-names and time-value names. They are merely other sets of musically hollow symbols that activate the decoding process. Without audiation, notation is marginal. Notation assists only in recalling what has been already audiated.

Experience in space audiation motion in improvisation makes boring and extended instruction in reading and writing music notation unnecessary. What musicians need to be explained to them is what they spatially audiate is what they see.

Early Childhood Music

As alluded to, change is difficult, and modifying pedagogy is no exception. Routine becomes more and more entrenched with advancing age of youngsters as well as adults. Thus, it makes sense to introduce young children to motion in space audiation and artistic sensitivity as soon as possible. They will mature with an intrinsic grasp of space audiation and therefore far-reaching need for change will become unnecessary.

A child learns more in the first eighteen months of life than in any other lifecycle period. Following are proposals for guiding newborns and older preschool children in space audiation motion as it is continuously embedded in their musical development. No attempt is made to introduce rules in terms of formal instruction. It is most advantageous for children to imitate one or more adults. That is to say there is no substitute for modeling by adults and peers.

A feeling for space motion is internalized and audiated by groups of children as they observe adults getting out of their own way and moving in space without inhibition. Recommended is continuous, free flowing movement using multiple parts of the body in unbound space. Brief unaccompanied songs and chants without words performed by adults are used. Words divert attention from movement and music. Various short periods of moving, singing, and chanting produce more beneficial results than one long period

Movement, not dancing or clapping, in stationary position or mobile is not regimented. Keeping musical time is avoided. It thwarts children's ability to realize motion in space audiation. Instrumental accompaniment and use of paraphernalia encourages time keeping. Children are not urged or directed to sing or chant. Above all, adults do not move in tandem with individual children by moving body parts for them. The goal is for children to observe, and possibly move if they so choose. There is no harm if children crawl but forcing them to walk before their time is unfavorable for their overall development.

There is a tendency for adults to keep time and accentuate macrobeats and microbeats when singing and chanting for children. This is most pronounced when moving parts of as well as the whole body. Rather than engaging in this action, adults best move in free, flowing circular movement without reference to musical time. Children are inspired to listen to short songs and chants in various tonalities, meters, and styles. Performances best incorporate ample space between and among macrobeats and microbeats for artistic renditions.

Given exposure to space audiation and early internalization of motion, children should easily and effortlessly become capable of participating in classroom music instruction and instrumental activities in elementary school. Recommended guidance will benefit adults as much as children.

Instruments

In the discussion of rhythm, space audiation was referred to as a template for musical time. Here, space audiation is explained as a template also for estimating physical distance when performing on a music instrument.

Consider, for example, string instruments, trombone, and piano. There are different positions for left hand when playing violin and string bass. Because many young violin students have no experience in motion in space audiation, a teacher attaches pieces of tape to a fingerboard indicating where fingers should be placed for various pitches. Even some professional string bassists have frets attached to the fingerboard of the instrument so their intonation may be more precise when playing in thumb positions. They, too, ostensibly have no sense of motion in space audiation. It seems tape and frets would be unnecessary if students and professionals were guided in sensing motion in space audiation preferably before they begin studying an instrument. Of course, it is never too late to attain a feeling of motion in space audiation, although ability to benefit from that insight diminishes with age.

Trombonists need to change slide positions to place most pitches. Some distances extend the length of an arm. With regard to piano, distances usually need to be estimated with both arms, hands, and fingers simultaneously. Undoubtedly determination of distances is involved in playing all music instruments, some needs being more obvious than others. Implications for distance in terms of space audiation may apply to length of bow to be used across a string depending on tempo and dynamics. Also, distance in conductors' arm spread may have a basis in motion in space audiation.

Whether feeling for physical distance safeguards pitch accuracy is a matter of speculation but it is more plausible than not that it does. It is also possible vocalists find it necessary to estimate distances relating to vocal folds for accuracy in pitch. Perhaps intonation is enhanced by feeling motion in space audiation.

Afterword

Music aptitude is influential in developing nuances related to motion in space audiation. A brief explanation of music aptitude follows.

Music aptitude is a measure of one's potential to learn music. It points beyond itself. Music achievement is a measure of what has been learned in music. For example, a person is not born knowing how to sing or play a music instrument. That must be learned, and once learned it is considered music achievement. Technical proficiency by itself, however, is not music achievement. It is simply skill for demonstrating music achievement, ideally embodied in audiation and applied to instrumental and vocal performance. In contrast, a person is born with more or less potential to learn how to perform music in a given style. That potential is considered music aptitude. Audiation is fundamental to music aptitude and consequently to spatial audiation in music achievement. Leaving instinct aside, consider intuition to be associated with music aptitude and insight with spatial audiation achievement.

Just as no person is void of at least some intelligence, no person is void of at least some music aptitude. To that extent everyone is musical. No one is incapable of learning to listen to and perform music with some degree of success. More than two thirds of persons are average. That is, they have average music aptitude. The remainder have above or below average music aptitude and very few have exceptionally high or low music aptitude. The results of valid music aptitude tests suggest approximately one or two in a hundred have exceptionally high music aptitude and only one in thousands has potential to achieve as a genius. Unfortunately, a substantial number of the minority who do may never be given proper recognition.

Amending pedagogy raises challenges. Understandably, it probably will not be effortless to implement even a portion of the information heretofore presented. Nevertheless, determination will prove to be well worth the effort. It should be reassuring that a mind exposed to a new idea cannot regain its original shape.

At one time music educators learned to teach. Now, it is time for them to teach to learn. That is especially true in terms of acquiring artistic ability in harmonic improvisation through motion in space audiation.

Bibliography

Edwin E. Gordon ....

BOOKS

Learning Sequences in Music: A Contemporary Music Learning Theory. GIA, Chicago, 2012.

Inseparability of Space and Time in Rhythm Improvisation. GIA, Chicago, 2014.

Rhythm: Contrasting the Implications of Audiation and Notation. GIA, Chicago, 2009.

Improvisation in the Music Classroom. GIA, Chicago, 2003.

Music Learning Theory for Newborn and Young Children. Chicago: GIA, 2013.

The Aural/Visual Experience of Music Literacy: Reading and Writing Music Notation.

GIA, Chicago, 2004.

Harmonic Improvisation for Adult Musicians. GIA, Chicago, 2005.

Clarity by Comparison and Relationship. GIA, Chicago, 2008.

Basics of Vocal and Instrumental Harmonic Improvisation. GIA, Chicago, 2013.

Essential Preparation for Beginning Instrumental Music Instruction. GIA, Chicago, 2010.

TESTS

Musical Aptitude Profile. GIA, Chicago, 1995.

Advanced Measures of Music Audiation. GIA, Chicago, 1989.

Harmonic Improvisation Readiness Record and Rhythm Improvisation Readiness Record. GIA, Chicago, 1998.

Appendix

The following presentation about design and construction of rhythm tests may be of current as well as historical interest.

Developmental period of *Musical Aptitude Profile* covered eight years, from 1957 to 1965, the date of its original publication. Many experimental tests were created during that time and reliability of each was judiciously examined. Thousands of students from around United States participated in the studies. Ultimately, it was decided to include seven tests in the music aptitude battery. Two are *Tonal -Melody and Harmony*; two, *Rhythm-Meter and Tempo*; and three, *Musical Sensitivity-Phrasing, Balance,* and *Style.* I will be referring specifically to rhythm tests.

For the *Meter* test, students are asked to compare pairs of short melodies that may or may not be in the same meter. If the answer is different, only meter changes. Melody remains constant. Students mark the same or different column for each question. For the *Tempo* test, students again are asked to compare pairs of short melodies that may or may not sound the same. If the answer is different, the ending of the second is performed faster or slower than the first. When the correct answer is same, both the statement and musical answer of each pair are re-recorded for both tests Thus, timbre is irrelevant. A classic study of validity of MAP, *The Longitudinal Predictive Validity of the Musical Aptitude* Profile, was published in 1967.

At least a dozen test tryouts were necessary to identify two rhythm aptitude tests that yielded substantial reliability. Acceptable tonal and musical sensitivity tests were more clearly evident. Ironically, unexpectedly the *Meter* test was found to be the best predictor of all seven MAP tests. That test came about as a serendipitous necessity because all virtual tests of rhythm had low reliability. The tentative rhythm tests evaluated included pairs of phrases of rhythm to be compared. Some phrases were eight macrobeats long and others four. Others had a tonal component. It was apparent a majority of students of all ages, musicians and non-musicians in grades 4 through 12, were not able to retain rhythm of the first phrase when listening to the second. That was the case regardless of meter and tempo. Comparing lengths of single durations was conclusively unreliable. I believe the *Meter* test is successful because rhythm is not an issue. Students need not listen to rhythm, only audiate overall context. That is, they need to distinguish between, for example, only duple and triple meters. Lengths of individual durations are of no concern.

In regard to *Tempo* test experiments, it was discovered most students were unaware of whether the same phrase, long and short and with or without tonal component, was performed at the same or different speeds. That was the case even when differences were extreme. High reliability was evident with only exaggerated alteration of speed of endings of phrases. At the time I did not give earnest thought to why some tests were impracticable. Now, with more than 50 years of experience, I think I have some answers. I will explain them in due course.

Harmonic Improvisation Readiness Record (HIRR) and *Rhythm Improvisation Readiness Record* (RIRR) were developed to gather objective information about how rhythm improvisation is learned and, using that information, how it might best be taught. Particular interests were understanding audiation of space and time relationships in improvisational potential and ability. Before their publication in 1998, validity of HIRR and RIRR was well established.

Harmonic Improvisation Readiness Record is a test of 43 pairs of harmonic patterns performed in various tonalities, all in the same uncomplicated rhythm. Directions for taking the test along with practice exercises are on the recording. Students are asked to listen to pairs of harmonic patterns and mark on an answer sheet whether two harmonic patterns in each pair sound the same or do not sound the same. If two patterns do not sound the same it is because chord progressions are different.

Rhythm Improvisation Readiness Record is a test of 40 pairs of space/time patterns, each pair performed with the same simple melodic line. Directions for taking the test along with practice exercises are on the recording. Students are asked to listen to pairs of space/time patterns and mark on an answer sheet whether the two in each pair sound the same or do not sound the same. If two patterns do not sound the same it is because two durations in the second space/time pattern are longer or shorter than in the first.

Means, standard deviations, and reliability coefficients for *Harmonic Improvisation Readiness Record* (HIRR) and *Rhythm Improvisation Readiness Record* (RIRR) were computed for elementary, middle, and high school groups and all groups combined. Results were astounding and seemed unbelievable. With regard to HIRR, there was less than half a point difference between means for elementary and high school students, and standard deviations were very close as well. There is less than one point difference between means for RIRR elementary and high school students, and standard deviations are also highly similar. Additional information about validity and related statistical matters are reported in the *Manual for Harmonic Improvisation Readiness Record and Rhythm Improvisation Readiness Record*.

Now with that background information, I feel confident I can concentrate on the main point. Until now, valid tests of rhythm, both aptitude and achievement, have persistently been arduous to design and implement. That is evident because although extant tests are titled rhythm tests, their content actually and necessarily comprises content other than rhythm. Consider MAP *Tempo* test. It measures awareness of speed as it requires less or more space. It does not relate to musical time or length of notes individually or collectively. In *Meter* test, context is emphasized rather than rhythm content. It was discovered direct or specific attention to traditional ideas of rhythm was unnecessary.

When the two tests were being finalized, I did not know why I was doing what I was doing. I knew only what I had to do. As I look back, what I have explained now seems clear. What musicians call rhythm and musical time are actually artifacts. Space is the compelling issue.

Thirty years or so after development of MAP, concepts became more self evident with development of HIRR and RIRR. I had to title RIRR a rhythm test because prepublication investigations revealed users would not understand what the test was if I used a title other than rhythm. Actually, it is a space test. In fact, the series of durations to be compared had to be called time patterns, not rhythm patterns, but in reality they are space/time patterns without links to musical time. There is a difference between musical time and natural time.

The questions in RIRR are comprised of short strings of durations without established meter. Students audiate amount of space and time between durations to determine relative lengths of durations. Audiation of continuous space, not musical time, is also the decisive point in HIRR. Patterns include three chords with the first and last always the tonic. The middle chord is the crucial one as it relates to audiation of a repetitive tonic. Rhythm is irrelevant but space and time are critical. There are two types of space. One is time of individual durations and the other time between individual durations.

There is a tangential thought related to space and time. I have reported there is less than half a point difference between HIRR means for elementary and high school students, and standard deviations are very close as well. Also, there is less than one point difference between means for RIRR elementary and high school students, and standard deviations are highly similar. These unique data, to my knowledge not found in any test of the same or different kind, are one of the reasons that lead me to believe *Harmonic Improvisation Readiness Record* and *Rhythm Improvisation Readiness Record* might be generic music aptitude tests. In both tests, space, not musical time, is measured. I believe there is compelling reason for music educators to dwell on space and non-musical time and give earnest attention to the foundation of music which is unfortunately but conventionally called rhythm.

Tunes for Space Audiation

Following are specially composed tunes particularly suited for emphasizing space audiation. They may be read or performed instrumentally or vocally in any style. Using them as a basis for space audiation improvisation would be advantageous.

Example 1.

Example 2.

Example 3.

Example 4.

Example 5.

Example 6.

Example 7.

Example 8.

Example 9.

Example 10.

Example 11.

Example 12.

Example 13.

Example 14.

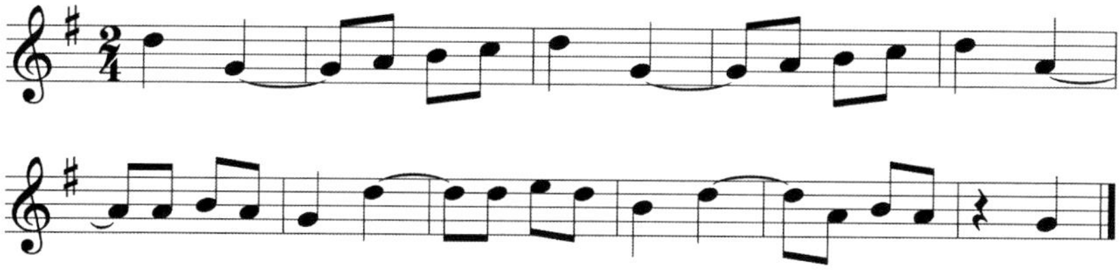

Example 15.

Example 16.

Example 17.

Example 18.

Example 19.

Example 20.

Example 21.

Example 22.

Example 23.

Example 24.

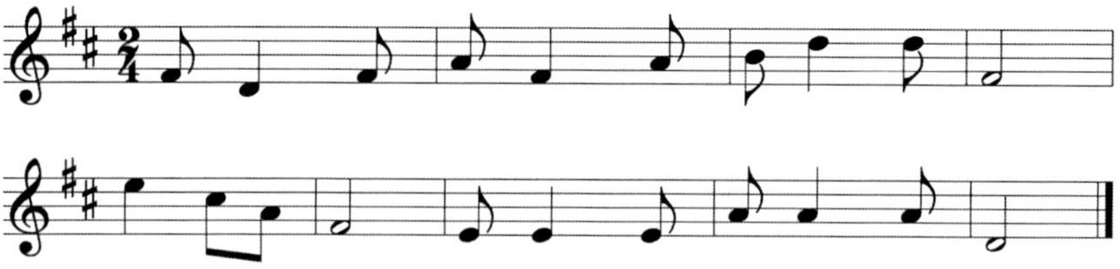

Example 25.

Example 26.

Example 27.

Example 28.

Example 29.

Example 30.

Example 31.

Example 32.